RED HAT AND NO

by

David Sowerby

Typeset and Published
by
The National Poetry Foundation
(Reg Charity No 283032)
27 Mill Road
Fareham
Hants PO16 0TH
(Tel: 0329 822218)

Printed by
Meon Valley Printers
Bishops Waltham (0489 895460)

Sponsored by Rosemary Arthur

Cover Photograph by Celia Rambaut

**In Rememberance
of my good friend Lilly Schluter**

ISBN 1 870556 91 7

CONTENTS

* * *

APRIL

April stands smiling at the window,
tears trickling down her face
in that moodswing phase
between girl and woman,
the prick of her budding hurting
in suddenness of sharp showers
and cloudy emotions
flooding across clear skies.

For April cruelty is not
the bursting of hyacinths out of the cold ground
but the wrench felt
by the delicacy of youth, the young year
becoming un-innocent, weary, summer blowsy
shaming the promise broken
by so many rainbows.

ASTRONAUTS

After the moon's violation,
a tin can of star sailors
hermetic against the night
probe under Virgo's girdle,
grope the ether
wary of black holes
and the awful gravity
of collapsed stars
which fail to shine.

The crew can never be fearful –
they've seen the worst;
the ordeal of men by men
on earth
more horrific by far
than monsters found
under the strange light
of an alien star.

ANEMONE CORM

Housed in this nonentity,
drab, wizened, dull
as dried rodent faeces,
posing as inorganic,
stonily arrogant,
fossil dumb as clay,
a red flower waits
for a rainstorm
like a late running 9X
to bring it home to
a coming out party.

AUTUMN LEAVES

Audrey, my next door neighbour,
positively hates nature.
Blind to the monstrosities of litter,
she simply loathes trees.

One morning after a night of gales,
she surveyed her svelte lawns
now speckled with random drifts of leaves,
those golden, bronze scarlet
failed promissory notes of
bankrupt summer.

"Are these yours?" she asks tartly.
I go along with her and reply,
"Er, this one is and that one,
but not those two."

Sensing my sarcasm,
she gives me a double barrelled blast
from her arctic blues.

I sigh and mutter darkly,
"Audrey, you are a bourgeois cow
and now you are shaking my tree hard
so that I long to drown you
in torrents of deciduous scarlet expletives
and stuff your livid knickers
with unseasonable holly!"

I turn away to fetch
my lawn rake, brush and barrow
to carry my errant children home.

OF BIRDMEN AND BUTTERFLIES

Once as a former birdman,
I flew, wrapped around by sixty tonnes
of shining metal and high octane fuel,
up among the stars in uncharted oceans
of air swept by fierce tides of wind
which brushed us from our homings.

Here, I sit at home under a buddleia tree
frequented by a stacking of admirals,
peacocks, tortoise-shells and green-veined whites,
all aerodynamically absurd as discarded toffee papers
but like me now, making no allowance
for drift of fickle winds and whimsies
where our minds might take us.

Under this indolent sun,
our E.T.A. is this very moment
as those two there over their target,
conjoined upon a flower
and I would swear
it's refuelling exercise
for further fluttery, coloured kites
to grace next summer's airways.

THE BIRDWOMAN COMETH

Over my shoulder I announce,
"Mother's coming to tea tomorrow"
and resume washing pots in the sink,
suitably absolved by detailed attention
to my task; wife groans, protests, but I
admonish, "try not to watch her eating,
chivvying, slicing, chasing food
around her plate."
Although my eyes too are drawn
like magnets to this annoying charade
and crave release from tension
when finally her hunted, harried food
has disappeared and
we relax with coffee.

I pause while washing a cup
and watch a blackbird on the lawn,
plunging, plucking out a worm,
chivvying it, slicing it, abandoning it,
taking it up again, chopping it, spreading it
and then beak upwards,
swallows it.

I smile, and guess
I know something about reincarnation.

COGNITO, ERGO SUM

I think, therefore I am –
this rule of thumb
postulated by Descartes
is wrong of course
in as much as he places
the wrong cart before the horse.

All evidence of life
is fundamentally more than this –
some of us do not think
but we are because we stink
which sets the organic apart
from the bedrock we lie on
and the water we drink.

Therefore mentally unwind,
apply deodorant liberally
with no thought in your mind
if you would become a non-entity.

But this thinker remains abashed
by the massive unthinking great unwashed
or the primpers and curlers and fops
and the rest of the asinine sansculottes.

DANDELION ALCHEMY

Take the bones of mountains
ground in a glacier's mortar
and in the earth's alembic
moistened with sea–sweat water
add an air–borne mote,
place under the sun's furnace
buring eight light minutes away
and from the serpent root diving
in the rich dark mould,
among the green leaves writhing
behold a crock of gold.

DEFENDANT OF THE TRUTH

Counsel for the prosecution remarked that
perhaps the defendant was economical with the truth,
a compliment I accepted with never a flinch
but secretly thought that truth's a
rare enough commodity to be splashing
about like deodorant for covering up
the real stink of life.

I got sent down for two years and was
duly thankful – out there, folk are
getting mugged for the cardboard coffins
they dossed down in,
warmth and regular meals
totally unknown.

Mind you, truth will out as they say.
In my case just one year, three hundred
and sixty-four days before it emerges
into the light of day,
the pearls of my convictions still shining
intact from the gathering swine.

DEEP DREAM DROWNING

When nightbergs thaw
and loose their meltwater light
through the closed curtains
to wash my eyes awake
on the gritty shore of another day,
I drowse and nuzzle in the surf
of sea foam dishevelled bed clothes
and feel a mermaid's hand
tumble me back in the undertow
of grey gloom breakers and drown happily again
in an ocean of dreams.

In a deep sea safe cave she sings
where the currents of time
run awry and hourglasses
empty silver sand on businessmen
in the guise of greedy crabs
asset stripping the corpses
of those whose ships of fortune
foundered on a bankrupt reef.

"Skulls," she says,
"have only two emotions;
boredom and malicious humour.
These eyeless bones were men,"
she says,
"who would not dream but toiled
and drowned in flood waves of reality."

Still pondering, I surface
when an alarm clock buoy
signals the presence of the other
world shoaling near.

DESERT

Rain was a new emotion
on the arid face of the desert,
the abandoned sarcophagi of
wrinkled seeds could not cope;
they split their sides laughing
in displays of coloured flags.

Mind you, that was seven years ago,
only an ant's walk around a
sundial in the scale of things.
Meanwhile other tombs of the dead
from that same ancient dynasty
strewn on the sand blowing
through the hourglass
of the shuffling dunes
await their resurrection
in the fulness of time-sent rain.

EAST MEETS WEST

Curiously east meets west
at St. Giles' church in a northern shire,
the Saxon tower squaring up to the centuries,
another year's leaves underfoot
among crumbling gravestones
and this morning, handsome Dr. Hassan
marries his fair English rose.

The bells peal out the news,
the low arc of light
sends the photographer scurrying,
light meter in hand,
searching for stray sunbeams.

The guests assemble over the dead
to be freeze-framed for posterity,
groom's family exotic in silken saris
glowing in Autumn gloom,
bride's folk more subdued in attire
reflecting Anglo-Saxon attitudes
at home in northern latitudes.

A white cat invites itself among legs,
one blue eye, the other orange
to illustrate that complimentary in liaison
odd arrangements work.
Cat chasing leaves,
blinking, wall eyed in the weak sunshine.

EMILY

My Wife's cousin Emily, twice removed,
(she used to live quite near)
enjoys a vain conceit which like a schoolgirl
she feels compelled to communicate
to her female peers.

She fondly imagines
that men from all walks of life
are mentally undressing her.

Pale, blonde and plain
in the middle of Marks and Sparks
I see her regaling my Wife again
how once more her femininity was stripped bare
to feed some random randy male's
prurient stare.

Bored, I hover on the fringes of her pantomime
of outraged sidelong glances, tossing hair
while affecting not to listen
until I am sufficiently irritated
to arrest this frivolous delay.

I turn and treat her to my deliberately
manufactured burning blue look
of unbridled lust and am amazed
to have it mirror-reflected
in her homely face.

Looking down suddenly,
I'm only wearing my ridiculous socks!

THE END OF SEASON EBB

On the sandbank
the sun catches the gulls
gleaming like daisies
which the restless tide
waits to mow away.

Far out, a dog,
dizzy with open space,
barks loudly,
borne faintly on the wind.

Near at hand,
an old man has found
some trinket in the sand;
lost, now found
and waiting to be
mislaid again.

Swingboats marooned
by the end of season ebb,
strain at their chains
remembering cargoes
of children carried
on the high seas of summer.

At the estuary mouth
vessels await the flood
to carry them up to
Grimsby, Hull and Goole,
over at Spurn
the stubbles are on fire.

ENVY, SELF SOWN

My competative muscle atrophied,
the Jones's next door have a clear field,
their drive crammed with power boat and skis.
Mr. Jones disappearing with golf clubs,
squash rackets regularly,
their house and garden acquiring
a grandeur putting ours in the shade
of their lilacs with somehow
they fail to notice, but we enjoy.

A gardener tends their flat lawns
and prissy borders once a week
but I am free from envy until
I notice a sky-blue flower
tumbling from a mortar joint,
self sown and unseen by anyone
which made me yearn to transplant
its favours in my own heart and home
but from that moment on something
stirred I hardly knew, a muscle
twitched somewhere shaping
a mouth with a hunger that
could grow into an insatiable maw.

A FELINE FANTASY

Tonight is a nocturne for cats,
velvet black and moth wing silky,
musky fragranted and underscored
to soaring swift's scream
diminuendo climbing aloft
allowing pipistrelle pizzicato
between the bowers
where I sit secretly
distilling felinity
from a mutant gland
which under the emergent stars
would have me on a rooftop
yodelling a lovesong
to a sickle-horned moon
in a boot-flung hailstorm
if I gave it free rein
from my composured adagio.

GOOSEBERRY BUSHES

The smiling young wife next door,
pregnant as a melon and overdue,
wears something like an old man's comb's,
donkey brown with contrasting yellow trim.
A most unbecoming garment, I think
but if she should explode
like the seed pods of Himalayan Balsam
while we're talking over the fence,
I think it might stretch a little further
to contain the twins or triplets
and the attendant giblets
from seeding manikins
under my gooseberry bushes.

FOR THE GRANDPARENTS

Watching my grandmother cleaning,
harrying the dust, feathers, cat hairs
and cobwebs to new locations,
I learned the mechanics of life.
Grandfather mucking the horses out,
pinching one nostril and volleying
snot among the midden
described the dynamics of ebb and flow.

Out of the dust and clay,
afterbirth and ordure,
fur, feather, scale and slime
form the rudimentary blocks
that shape a bird that sings,
a flower that exults in scent and hue
and nonetheless I also have my hour
in which I savour a shiver of fulfilment
before extinction as
those aged pair who obscurely
handed down my inheritance of blood
from the remote marriage bed
they youngly twisted and delighted in.

Now they are bounden graveward
spent as toppled oaks
to feed the questing roots of trees
silently budding in the churchyard.

In church close
I looked at the corpse of a lamb
squirming in death with
a million maggots
and I tell you, Brother,
we are sad music and dust
falling in ancient sunlight.
What wisdom we have learned
are words smudged by tears.

THE GRAND EPIC PRODUCTION

I'd like you to know that I'm starring
in a Grand Epic Production.
Well, not actually starring but a 'walk on' bit
of all too brief duration.
Still, I think I would rather be a 'bit extra'
than cast as a deaf musician or blind painter.

The production is many stories within a story
and I'm told the dying scenes are right out of this world.
Some say it is all camp, just a grand farce
whilst others see it as high drama
and one point of view is that it is a musical.
I must admit I'm rather puzzled all the way through
and unable readily to grasp the plot myself.

I was cast in my part by three women;
they call themselves the Present, Past and Future.
Being of limited aptitude
I never got near to the Producer or Director.
Both Jewish of course.
The Producer went by name of G.Hovah and
the Director was J.Christ.
But of course he was relatively newly appointed.
There had been several others from the start
of the Production.

The Prompter was a certain B.L.Zeebub,
another Jew but a person with quite a turn of charm
and it is rumoured secretly that he hopes to succeed
as Director,
to which many of the cast would give their acclaim

I really must be moving along,
the next scene is a holocaust, a war or fire or flood
or something.
See you back in the dressing room.

A GRIMSBY NIGHTINGALE

My friend who sips life so casually
and allows herself to become
mildly drunk in the process,
rapturously insists that
close to midnight on New
Year's Eve she listened
to a nightingale singing
in busy, tree-lined Bargate,
although as a know-all
naturalist, I could have
told her that the birds
sit out our winter in Africa
when only robin sings at home
and was probably woken by
street lights from bushy dreams
to believe in a sunrise
beyond his means.

Perhaps I am too kind not
to disillusion her fond fantasy
but wise enough to encourage
her inclinations in the hope
that one day she will
disabuse my cynical science
by rediscovering a unicorn,
lured by her spiritual virginity
in Weelsby Woods,
for her whimsical suppositions,
it seems, grow on trees
and as such are
eminently biodegradable

FELLOW TRAVELLERS

Perhaps something in the face,
my patient passive reverie,
tells the stranger as I wait
in some other town's public place
that here's a good listener
clad opportunely in anonymity
to be father confessor
for the burden of some sin or slight
and so they offload on this miserable toad
the things that keep them awake at night.

What sister had accused
after mother was laid to rest
or how now, redundant, aimless,
they feel at loss,
out of face with wife,
bullied by the boss,
generously they get it off their chest.

Unloosing such bottled up strife on me
who can only make sympathetic noises,
offer what wisdom and kindness I can
then shoulder my own weighty neuroses,
mixed guilt and painful hurt
to follow the road they travel
sometimes not seeing the roses
but equally weary and worn,
spoiled by the same dust and dirt.

IN THE THINKER'S ARMS

In the Thinker's Arms, my friend, Bryan,
the well–informed engorger of knowledge
as disseminated by the New Scientist
and Sunday Times, modern replacement
authorities for the Bible,
quotes floods of facts and statistics.

I interupt him and ask, "what do you
want the figures to say, Sir?"
He pauses momentarily, gives me a funny look,
slakes his irritation from my acidity
with another long sip of beer.

I want to ask him why he is ashamed
of his own children, his own free–born
thoughts that he will not back his hunches.
Are they too deformed for public appearance
that he has to adpot foundling clones of thought
which he fosters along with so many others?

I see the future and it hurts!
Comes the day when we are drinking
in the Union Jack Pub and our conversation
drowned out by the other topers
reciting statistics from the National Times
with the Thought Police hunting
me among the throng for voicing
my dissident 'View Halloo's' of
the foxy thoughts I might unleash
to scatter and alarm these complacent
chickens, safe behind their wire netting
protection of the state guarding them
from a reality too unthinkable.

KRISTINA

Madam, I have seen your
cool professionalism slip
on a long banana skin of anger
thrown underfoot by the
passing heat of the moment.
I watched you tumble base
over apex showing your
so-correct, directoire
pink knickers.

What made me laugh was to
see among the embroidered
flowers, there was this
word, 'Humility' picked
out in red letters
across the arse.

I am, in case I should slip too,
able to proffer a warm hand
on which there is tattooed
the slogan 'Forgiveness'
in almost unreadably
small print although by
a trick of the light
it may look like 'Gloating',
I am ready to restore
your ruined equilibrium.

LITTLE EVA

Parson John traced
the sign of the cross
in holy water
on my elfin skull.
The schoolmaster
poured hard facts
through my pixie lugs.
The doctor chased
crops of spots
from the white field
of my fairy body
but it was Little Eva
behind the school
bikeshed, with
her marbled thighs
and navy blue knickers
who taught me how
sweet stolen red
apples tasted.

FOR MAX AND POLLY

This is a house where cats
are treated with sanctity
accorded to Hindu cows.
In the morning having made my bed,
they lie on it.
Asleep on the coverlet
they borrow from dogdom
the caveat not to be woken.

Hoovering   postponed,
a radio symphony respectfully
turned down low,
this house a temple
to Lady Bast of ancient Egypt;
my fat cats mummified in kindness.

Their world full of enemies
to be killed or seduced by charm.
When they die,
I fear I may do something silly
like shaving off my eyebrows.

MAX

Max, sturdy and fat
extrovert, boisterous bear,
more cuddly bruin than cat
solicits fingers
to tickle
his bellyroll fur.

Cons old ladies
in pensioners' flats
wailing pathetically
to sit on various
fireside mats
for something like
tea and sympathy.

Rolls home
in immaculate
evening dress
to fussily compare
whether the fish
we serve
is fresh or
as good as that
elsewhere.

MONUMENTAL ARROGANCE

The phrenology of landscape
in this flat place
placed two hillocks
on our coastal plain.
One where this house now stands
overlooking the other where
Neolithic man burnt his dear and dead
and tidily stored their ashes
in a clay jar buried in the mound
that tops the hill.

Changes since his day
have let the sea eat more land,
claim the oaken forest where
he hunted wild boar and at
one time an Elizabethan beacon
blazed a warning on his barrow
when Armada threatened.

A town has mushroomed round it now
and his urns disinterred this century
glower in glass cases in the library
where the past and present mingle
and mutely offer some warning
of pages yet unwritten
that will chronicle our raising of a mound
of foulness, waste,
built as a monument
to our arrogant technology.

MY FRIEND ERIC

My friend Eric, the master forger
steals woodland vistas with his eyes,
flogs them to landlocked townies
who survive the brick-built drabness
with his couterfeits of nature
framed on their parlour walls.

In law he is irreproachable,
only guilty of some sleight of hand and eye
whereby he stains a paper with some simple dye
so your mind may enter field or grove
allowing your displacement
to feel a little more like home.

MY GIDDY COUSIN

My giddy cousin,
many times removed from reality,
imagines herself femme fatale,
sends messages with her eyes
across public rooms
searching for romance,
perhaps where seafarers congregate
and have learnt the lingua franca
of sexual availability in various
scattered international bars,
lusty men who blench
over their intoxicants,
interpreting mental derangement,
epilepsy, even strangulated
hernia in such a pretty girl,
my beautiful, empty-headed cousin
in her passionate grimaces.

MYSTERY TOUR

He boarded our bus,
brash and cocky with superior wit,
wearing his badges of wealth,
a tall stetson, enormous buckled leather belt
and a necklace of expensive cameras,
the middle-aged American with his wife
dressed in a freakish, puce trouser suit
and matching hat
over a face burnt by Californian sun
to the texture of a seamy, leather handbag.

She remained aloof behind
large framed, bejewelled spectacles
but the Yank kept up a loud barrage
and aired his extrovert personality.
We were forced to generate denser clouds
of English reserve until
we entered quiet winding lanes
where the beeches and oaks met overhead
to filter the June sun
and throw a shadowy dapple
on the lush verges of Queen Anne's lace,
cow parsley, hogweed and modest wild rose
rambling and festooning the hawthorne hedgerows
planted centuries before by our Saxon fathers.

The gaps in the tree tunnel
yielded views of pied Friesians
cropping buttercup-spangled turf
and remote farmsteads with
pantile roofs huddling close
to greystone Mother Curch.
The Yank, exotic and cactus bold
from sun-scorched, semi-deserts
and luxurious air conditioning,
breathed almost inaudibly
"Gee! this is really somephun."

I began to warm towards him.

OLD GRIMSBY

In the days of my youth,
'red hat and no drawers',
rang the cry on the streets
signifying a loose woman.
Now I titter with middle-aged imaginings
at haute couture, sophisticated young biddies
scarlet-hatted, in oblivion to old meanings.

Where are the girls who clamoured
like brassy gulls when the fishing fleet docked
spilling crans of herring and lusty crews
on a two day holiday spending spree
from the grey grimness of the North Sea;
Dollar Princess, Russian Rabbit, Green Linnet,
Mud May and hare-lipped Nellie Ming Mong?

Poor lisping Nellie who produced in a fish and chip shop,
two pennies disguised in silver paper
proffered her as furtive payment
under some ghastly gaslight,
who at remonstrance uttered for apocrypha,
"Well, I'll be blowed, fucked me for tuppence!"

Laughter and Hewitt's Best Bitter
at the 'Barrel', 'Red Lion' and 'Lincoln'
whilst vessels were floundering in wastes of waves
to send the port missioner to the wives of sea dead.
Young widows bereft, with strings of kids,
wearied beyond years, taking in washing,
poverty widespread – but doors unlocked!
And yet old Grimsby laughed
while now it sulks, the fishing gone
and the good, bad old days, so generously hard
have followed the trawler fleet
to the breaker's yard.

THE NATURAL HISTORY MASTER

He talks the language of dead birds,
stuffed owls, glass-cased golden orioles,
dusty dodos and swan skins.
Why can't he listen to
the larks behind the bus shelter,
observe the long-legged, hairy-bearded twit
stalking the voluptuous strutting
of the greater, big-girl's blouse,
the ring-nosed, punk cockerel's flagrant display
or study the furious mating urges
of the lesser-spotted herberts
he has caged in detention
for wolf-whistling the pretty dinner lady;
the one with a short skirt,
legs long as ostrich's
bossoms fluttery as a sage grouse,
happy among admirers?

ON PUTTING ONESELF OUT OF THE WAY
ACCORDING TO ZEN

Intent on oblivion I climbed a high tree
to fix a rope to manufacture for myself
eternity's   pendulum.
Ascending, I had qualms about falling.

With a whetted knife hungering for my wrist
to bring about a red fountain of no tomorrows,
I found myself pondering on the likelihood
of infection.

Again, wading in the cold unfriendly sea
seeking to savour the breath of fishes
and dreamlessness in the deeps,
I brooded with disquiet on my future putresence.

Now in the cold ground,
unresponsive under the sod,
I crave awareness.
Awakening, tooth–ache might be such ecstacy.

OUT OF THE MOUTHS OF BABES...

Foul-mouthed at four years old,
his parents think he's cute.
He told me indecorously
to be about my way.
My Victorian upbringing rebuked
his Anglo-Saxon to which (I thought)
he gave me some misplaced cub's salute.

Well meaningly, I told him never
to use those words again
but on reflection later
I felt they might be justified
when Jehovah's Witnesses at the door
summon you out of the bath.
There's some satisfaction in profanity
I admitted wryly to myself
with a small derisory laugh.

THE PAST IS ANOTHER COUNTRY

Never return to that happy place
you found while journeying,
the old inn with cockly tables
chattering on an uneven floor
where cold beer flowed
in a gloom hidden from
the hot day's clout
among buzz of soft talk
floating amid the flies
about prospects of weather
and early harvest.

Now liveried flouncy girls
smiling their 'nice day' smile
serve fizzy lagers brewed
by chemists in white coats
somewhere down the motorway
and loud brittle chatter
merges with a frantic African drum
brute bawling some incomprehensibility.
Instead make good your escape
and weave between the status symbols
on the car park where they
bulldozed the stables away
for this is where they
are building Babel anew,
the past is another country
you only thought you knew.

PRAISE THE LORD

Praise the Lord, it was Sunday
when thrush songsmith hammered out
his hymn on the anvil of the dawn.

Later on Radio Four
a church broadcast with angelic
choirs was purely secondary
in excellence.

On the streets, neighbours
washed cars, trimmed lawns;
still thrush sang on.

While oily starling hordes
squabbled over the splattered pizza
of some previous night reveller's vomit.

The world at one, I thought.

POACHER

Long tails, ring necks, lordly pheasants
posing in woodland and meadow,
skulkers of leaf–shady keepered coverts;
I tell them they have no place here
as I do.

My pedigree, if it should show,
would be a predatory livery of bands and stripes,
armorial of a chequered career
of living by stealth within the heart of land
just as my brothers in crime,
strung up, stinking on the gibbet;
weasel, stoat, fox, hawk,
falcon, owl and even pussycat.

We are part of the English scene
not introduced as this stubble strutter,
cossetted proud cock.
Brimming with bitter injustice
that liberty, equality and fraternity
never did catch on,
I look down my nose and gun barrel,
then hammer cocked, I blast him
muttering for the swinging dead,
"*Morte aux Aristo!*"

A sadness as I retrieve
this Sun King's ruin
of bronze, gold, blue-black, scarlet finery
but hearing the keeper's dog,
I clutch corpse, gun, bag and all
and run past mantraps and malice
to dine as well as those up at the Hall,
whom a form of unnatural selection
has chosen to be my betters.

PRAYING MANTIS

Whilst locked in copulation
the female praying mantis
is said to devour her suitor.

Erika, the rector's daughter
noted for striking attitudes
of piety and devotion
taught me that the male
doesn't necessarily care
too much.

RAINBOW WISHES

Rain, rain swallocking down,
resentful, bitter, winter rain,
the old stained, grey blanket
thrown up at the sun's window,
gargling down bottomless,
yawning gargoyle gullies,
washing the earthworm out;
enough is enough!.

Pock mark the dust elsewhere,
deluge blotting paper deserts,
there, slake the withered seed
to flower brimful,
flashflood the thirsty plain,
bring choirs of frogs,
soak the earth's sour mouth
where it needs you
or refrain
and take sunlight,
go clothe yourself
in rainbow bloomers.

RIVERS UNDER THE TOWN

Rivers flow under this town
nor will be denied
their ancient courses
judged by hill and fold
allotted by post-glacial meltdown.

They still struggle and wind
despite obstructual difficulties
posed by humankind
to bear their raindrop tribute
to the open sea.

Freshney, Haven, Redhouse
and Goosepaddle,
once lisping sweetness
bordered with reedmace
marigold garlanded
skirted with willow
sponged the marshland.
Now prisonered in darkness
they mutter in culverts,
sullen
and foul.

But despite traffic overhead
they still flow
in the subconscious of this town,
sluggish and silent
into the murky Humber's rebellious thoughts.

ROSEMARY COTTAGE

After your hospitality
the happy guest returning home
ventured in an ungracious moment
unguarded by wine,
"Why Rosemary Cottage,
where is the rosemary?"

Unobserved, it scented the
evening air away
from the gated drive
and your answer was
to pluck a sprig and
proffer it for remembrance
where it now blooms in my garden
reminding me of your gentleness,
my brash questioning
that spiked the evening
somehow like a quarrelsome thistle
when I should have been sage enough
to have given you thyme.

THE SINGER AND HIS SONG

The thrush, which to my delight
had sung all week when
blacky and redbreast were dumb,
today is missing,
has not come
but later underneath the pear
I found his ruffled corpse
bedraggled   there
and knew the cat I also loved
had got his tongue.

A SMALL SANCTITY IN THE RAIN

Today I saw a tableau of men
garbed in the tattered poverty
of saints,
wild–haired, eyes of holy icons,
priests of oblivion
grouped in a cobbled alley
just off the main street,
gulping down forgetfulness
in an embrace of dulled feeling
against unbelonging
and the cold rain.
Hardly a ritual
of voluptuous Bacchanalians,
more a break–away
protestant movement
in which I understood
the piety of their cause
but turned away because
I was too unworthy
to become a novitiate.

SOUR GRAPES

My rich relations borrow
exotic sunlight,
search for Golden Fleeces;
and 'New', 'Improved', 'Instant' hype
whilst I beggerly become
their unpaid janitor
guarding opulent house,
prissy gardens
against the thief in the night
or by day (if he has the gall)
perhaps with whom I share
a sense of deprivation
and unbelonging
but duty bound I cope
but cannot hinder
corruption of dust,
frail moths
as the Biblical Savant foretold,
meanwhile I sleep in drabness,
try to spin dreams of gold
from common bedstraw
until they bring me my reward;
a bottle of foreign plonk
that would cure an alcoholic
thirsting in the Gobi.